My Water Comes From The Mountains

by **Tiffany Fourment**

illustrated by **Dorothy Emerling**

ROBERTS RINEHART PUBLISHERS
in cooperation with
The Institute for Arctic and Alpine Research
University of Colorado

This book was prepared through the Niwot Ridge Long Term Ecological Research project of
the Institute of Arctic and Alpine Research at the University of Colorado, in recognition of
the International Year of Mountain. The author, Tiffany Fourment, participated in an alpine
ecology field course taught by Prof. Diane McKnight at the Mountain Research Station.

The book includes text and illustrations by students in the author's third grade class at
Friends School in Boulder, Colorado. Support for the book was provided by the K-12
Schoolyard Program of the Long Term Ecological Program of the national Science
Foundation.

Roberts Rinehart Publishers
An imprint of The Rowman & Littlefield Publishing Group, Inc.
4501 Forbes Boulevard, Suite 200
Lanham, MD 20706

Distributed by NATIONAL BOOK NETWORK

Library of Congress Card Number: 2003022734
ISBN: 1-57098-387-9 (cloth : alk. paper) ; 1-57098-388-7 (pbk. : alk. paper)

∞™ The paper used in this publication meets the minimum requirements of American
National Standard for Information Sciences—Permanence of Paper for Printed Library
Materials, ANSI/NISO Z39.48-1992.

Manufactured in the United States of America.

One day, way up in the Rocky Mountains of Colorado, snow fell softly to the ground.

"What's the big deal about that?" you ask. Snow falls all the time in the Rocky Mountains—but do you know what happens to the snow after it's on the ground? Any guesses? Yes, it melts and turns into water, and that very same snow that falls in those mountains is what comes out of our faucets. When we get a drink of water, take a bath, or turn on the sprinklers in our yard, we are drinking, bathing, and watering our grass with snow.

Sound strange? Well, if you've ever wondered where your water comes from, how it gets there, or where it goes after we use it, read on, and follow water's journey through a watershed as it changes from the fluffy white snow we see in the mountains to the clear liquid we use everyday.

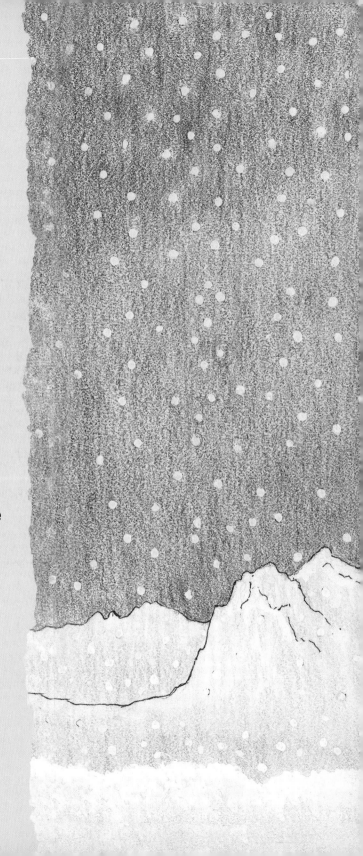

Before we start this journey, though, there is one big question: what exactly is a *watershed*?

A watershed is an area of land where water collects. The water runs down the mountains and hills into the valley bottoms. The watershed includes not only the river or lake where the water ends up, but the land that the water runs through on its way there. So what does this mean? Well, much like when a dog sheds its hair during the summer, for instance, the mountains and hills "shed" water after it snows or rains.

The Continental Divide, for example, is a boundary for many watersheds, including the Boulder Creek watershed. Much like a big bowl that collects water from the surrounding mountains and hills, this watershed is the area of land in and around Boulder, Colorado, and nearby cities, where water from many streams and lakes comes together. If you live near one of these cities, the Boulder Creek watershed is your source of water.

—Maia Bishop-Bondestam

WHAT IS THE BOULDER WATERSHED?

"The watershed is a place where we get our water from. Some of our water comes from the Arapahoe Glacier. The watershed is a place where all the water starts to collect in one place." —Alexa Pesenti

—Chloe Sens

THE CONTINENTAL DIVIDE

"What is the Continental Divide? It is part of the Rocky Mountains. It divides watersheds all around the country. If it rains, the rain goes east or west."

—Maddy Hemmeter

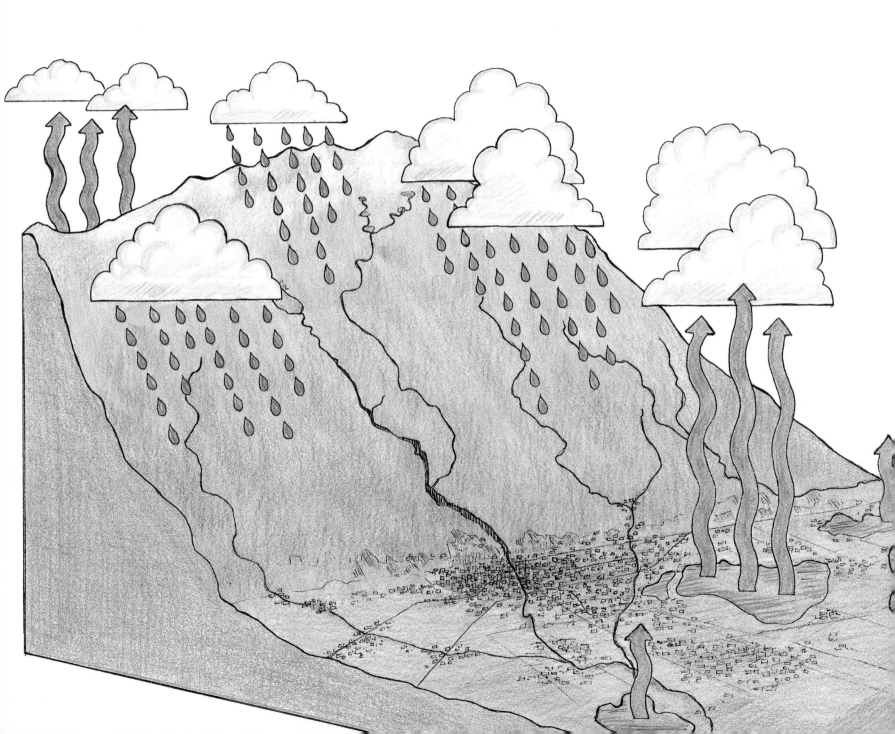

All the water on Earth is part of one big cycle and the journey of water through our watershed is only a small part of that cycle. Throughout the whole planet, the sun's heat makes water evaporate from oceans, lakes, and streams. As the water vapor rises in the air, it cools off and makes clouds. When the clouds get heavy with moisture, the water falls back to the Earth as rain or snow. This water collects again in an ocean, lake or stream that may be far away from where it evaporated from in the beginning. Of course, as we will see, water can go through many different stages in its journey, but regardless if it's vapor or snow or rain, it is always part of Earth's water cycle.

Now that you know a little bit about water and watersheds, let's take a trip through the Boulder Creek watershed.

"The water in the world, including the Boulder watershed, was placed there at the beginning of the world, and is still here today. The water evaporates, and then snows, rains, or hails down again. Even when you drink water, the water goes back to the earth, so the water we have is the same water that was on the earth the first day the planet was formed."

—Jorin Becker

The journey of water through our watershed begins way up in the mountains west of Boulder, Colorado. Here, the snow that falls in the winter collects on the ground and waits for the warm spring sun to melt it. Snow also collects on the Arapahoe Glacier, which is a large field of snow and ice located in the mountaintops of Green Lakes Valley. It's another source of water for the watershed.

But . . . it's so cold up here on these big fields of snow and ice that, even during the hottest days of the summer, only a tiny bit of the glacier melts. Talk about long-lasting snowfall! In the winter, the snow builds up on the glacier so much that it never gets a chance to melt. That's why it is there year after year, and you and I can see snow-covered mountains even in the middle of summer!

WHAT IS THE ARAPAHOE GLACIER?

"Arapahoe Glacier is a glacier in the Rocky Mountains near Boulder. Some of our water in Boulder comes from Arapahoe Glacier."   —Thomas Irvine

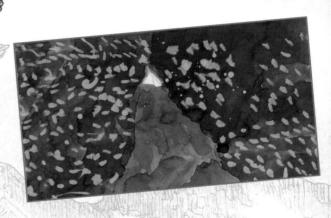

"Boulder is the only city in the United States that owns a glacier."   —Wes Mason

In the spring, as the snow starts to melt on the glacier, and on the mountaintops and piles of large rocks, called talus, the snowmelt trickles downward through the alpine tundra. Because it is so cold and windy on the highest part of the mountains, not many plants and animals can survive in the alpine tundra.

"There are very high winds in the mountains of the Boulder watershed area. Any wind above 70 miles per hour is considered a hurricane. At heights, there is a very strong wind called the jet stream."

—Jordan Bedell

There aren't any trees that live here, because the high winds and cold temperatures are too much for them. The plants that do grow in the alpine tundra grow in small clumps and very close to the ground, where they are more protected from the wind. This is why some people say it looks like a desert—because the trees have deserted!

"Try this on a windy day, go outside and stand as tall as you can, with your arms stretched up, and then crouch low to the ground and make yourself as small as you can."

—Maia and Linn
Bishop-Bondestam

Only a few animals live in the alpine tundra year-round. They are the yellow-bellied marmot, pika and white-tailed ptarmigan (pronounced tar-mi-gan) to name a few. Water drips and trickles through the rock fields on the alpine tundra that are home to the pika, a small creature that looks like a chubby squirrel without a long tail. CHEEP CHEEP—As the pika scurries among the rocks, its high-pitched call sounds almost like a bird chirping.

SNOW

"In the winter, the trees hold the snow. So, in the summer, all the snow turns to water to drink. If we had less snow, it would affect our water supply in Boulder."

—Harper Dilts

THE WHITE-TAILED PTARMIGAN

"The White-Tailed Ptarmigan changes color. In the winter it is white and in the summer it is brown. The white-tailed ptarmigan is the only bird that can live in the alpine tundra all year round."

—Hunter Jorgensen

As the water continues downhill from the alpine tundra, it flows through patches of twisted, funny-looking trees that grow close to the ground. These trees, called krummholz, grow in very special ways that help them to survive. Because they grow very high up on the sides of the mountains (sometimes over 11,000 ft in elevation), they grow sideways with the treetops pointing away from the wind. In fact, some of these trees are hundreds of years old, and they only come up to your knees!

FLAGGING

"Since winds are rough in the high mountains, trees do something called flagging. That's when the branches grow on one side of the tree, the side that does not get hit by the wind."
—Isa Mazzei

KRUMMHOLZ

"The krummholz are trees that can't grow because of ice and wind. They grow on the edge of the alpine tundra."
—Nathaniel Johnson

As the water keeps flowing downward, it enters a forest of larger, more "normal-looking" trees, like the ones you see everyday. Since they don't live in harsh windy conditions, like the krummholz, they grow taller and straighter. In this forest, the water that has been trickling along the ground starts to collect in small streams and ponds. This is where animals such as the pine marten, the snowshoe hare, the mountain lion, and birds of all shapes and sizes come along to take a drink.

SNOWSHOE HARE

"The snowshoe hare is white in the winter and brown in the fall, spring, and summer. It lives in the subalpine region."

—Abbey Yaron

THE GREAT HORNED OWL

"The Great Horned Owl is one of the many birds that live in the subalpine zone. The Great Horned Owl has long, fringed wings with sound-deadening filaments at the tips of the flight feathers."

—Josh Crist

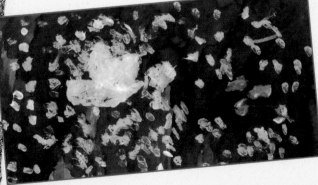

From these small streams and ponds, the water starts to flow into larger ponds and streams as it moves down from the mountains toward our city—Boulder. Most of these streams flow into two major reservoirs. They are the Barker Reservoir and the Lakewood Reservoir. A reservoir is a large, man-made lake with a dam at one end that traps the water until it is needed. These two reservoirs store the water that runs into them. Some of the water from the reservoirs flows into even larger streams and some goes through a pipe to a water treatment facility.

At the water treatment facility, the water is treated to make it okay for people to drink. Water that is not piped to the treatment plant is released into North Boulder Creek and Middle Boulder Creek and continues to flow downstream.

OUR WATER SUPPLY

"I am in the mountains and I hold a lot of our water supply. Am I Barker Reservoir or Boulder Reservoir? Answer: Barker Reservoir. Boulder Reservoir is in the plains and holds some of our water supply too."

—Michael Head

With a crashing ROAR, the water in North Boulder Creek pours and splashes over Boulder Falls and flows into Middle Boulder Creek, forming Boulder Creek. The water in Boulder Creek continues to flow downstream, rushing through the canyon.

Many plants and animals such as fox, coyotes, and chipmunks live in this area. They depend on Boulder Creek and the smaller streams that run into it for food, water, and shelter. Oh look! A deer that has been grazing nearby has gone down to the water for a drink.

BIRDS IN THE MONTANE ZONE

"In the montane area there are many birds. Two of them are the Great Horned Owl and the woodpecker."

—Berkeley Fial

MULE DEER

"Deer graze in the montane meadows. They are especially fond of the aspen groves, where they nibble on the trees and leaves."

—Maddie Filderman

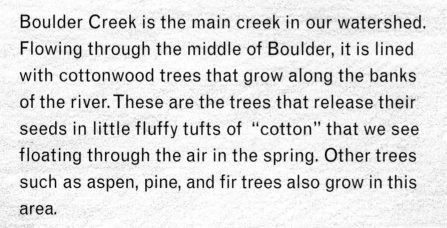

—Linn Bishop-Bondestam

SPLASH !

Boulder Creek is the main creek in our watershed. Flowing through the middle of Boulder, it is lined with cottonwood trees that grow along the banks of the river. These are the trees that release their seeds in little fluffy tufts of "cotton" that we see floating through the air in the spring. Other trees such as aspen, pine, and fir trees also grow in this area.

A kayaker paddles through the cold, fast-moving water of the rapids in the creek.

People use Boulder Creek for many things too. Some like to fish, swim, or float in the creek. But have you ever felt the water in Boulder Creek? It's very cold—in early summer, the water can be almost as cold as ice—Brrr! That's just like playing in the snow, because, that's right, it is snow!

Now, remember the water that was piped into the treatment facility from the Barker and Boulder Reservoirs? Well, that water is the same water that trickled down from the mountains high above the city and now comes out of our faucets and hoses. The only difference is that it has been treated to make it clean for us to drink.

WHERE DOES IT GO?

When you drain the bathwater out of your tub after a bath, what happens to it? Water that we use in our toilets, sinks, and showers ends up in the sewer and is piped to a different kind of treatment facility, where it is cleaned and released back into Boulder Creek. Some water, like the water that runs down the sides of the street after a big rain, runs directly into Boulder Creek through storm drains.

As the water continues on its trip down Boulder Creek, the land starts to change again. The pine and fir trees disappear, as the creek flows through a prairie. Yippp yipp yipp, YEOWWWW . . . a coyote's call is answered by another.

There are not many trees on the prairie, mostly just grasses that can survive the dry weather here. Animals such as prairie dogs, ferrets, burrowing owls, and antelope live on the prairie, and yes, you guessed it, they depend on the creek for water too!

FERRETS

"Ferrets live in the prairie life zone. Ferrets kill prairie dogs, and they live in the prairie dogs' homes. Black-footed ferrets are on the Endangered Species list."

—Sarah Gager

BURROWING OWL

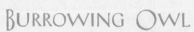

Farmers who also live on the prairie depend on the creek to irrigate their crops. Irrigation means using water from somewhere else to water crops where there is not enough rainfall for the crops to grow. In fact, the corn that you buy at the Boulder Farmers' Market might have been grown with water from the very same creek that you're reading about in this book!!

Some fertilizers that help the corn grow faster, or chemicals that keep bugs from eating the corn, can dissolve into the irrigation water. This water then goes back into the creeks and rivers. In towns, there are pollutants that can get into creeks like Boulder Creek. These pollutants can come from runoff from roads or chemicals applied to lawns.

—Linn Bishop-Bondestam

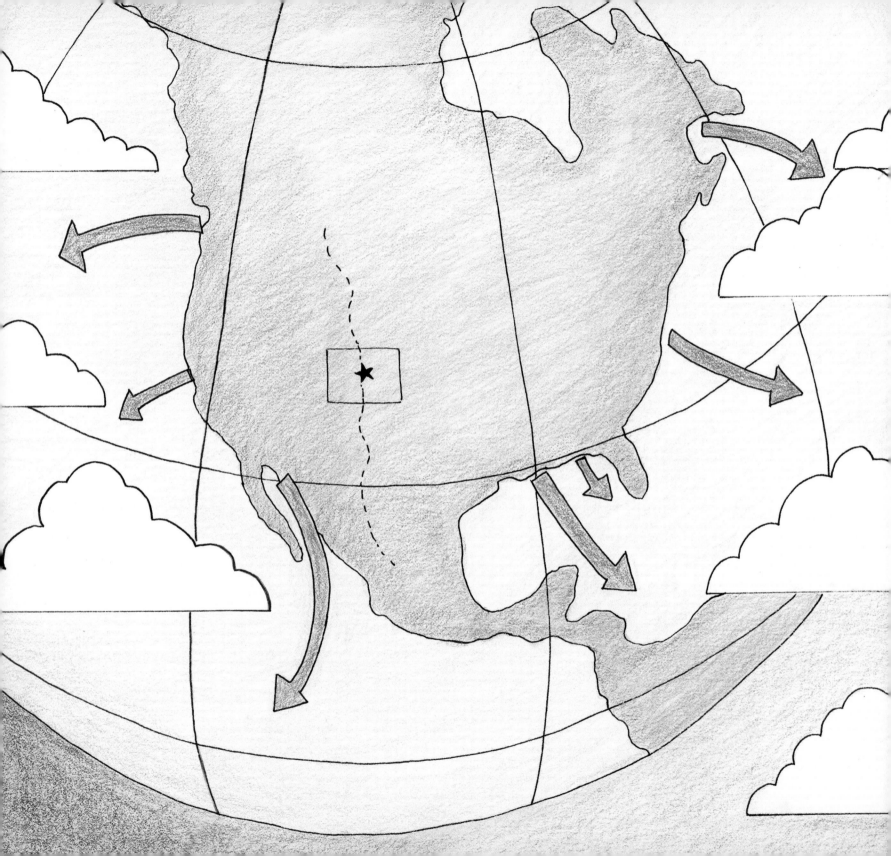

As the creek flows through the prairie, beyond the city of Boulder, it meets up with the St. Vrain River, which has its own watershed located north of the Boulder Creek Watershed. As the two creeks join, the water continues its journey, flowing next into an even larger river, the South Platte River, and then eventually reaching the Mississippi River, one of the longest rivers of the world. From there it runs all the way to the Gulf of Mexico and the Atlantic Ocean. And when it gets there, what do you think happens then?

That's right! As the sun rises in the sky to warm the new day . . . the water cycle starts all over again. Some of it evaporates out of the ocean, then it collects as clouds, and, eventually, when it gets cold enough, it snows. And way up in the mountains, the Rocky Mountains to be exact, snow falls softly to the ground.

"I am part of the water cycle that is part of the Boulder watershed. I am mistaken for air sometimes. What am I? Answer: Water vapor."   —Annie Saltonstall

THE CONTINENTAL DIVIDE

"If it rained on top of the Continental Divide, it would eventually go to the Pacific Ocean or to the Atlantic Ocean. When it goes to the west, it goes to the Pacific Ocean. When it goes to the east, it goes to the Atlantic Ocean."

—Carrie Dean

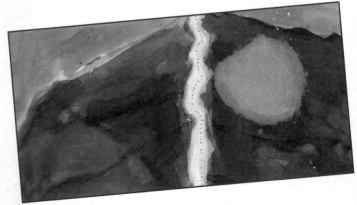

ABOUT THE AUTHORS

Tiffany Fourment is an environmental educator who has taught at Friends School in Boulder, Colorado, as well as at the Wild Bear Nature Center in nearby Nederland. She currently teaches in Costa Rica.

Dorothy Emerling is a freelance illustrator who has illustrated all six books in the Wild Wonders series (Roberts Rinehart/Denver Museum of Nature and Science).

The publisher and authors would like to thank the following Boulder-area third graders for their contributions to this book:

Jorin Becker
Jordan Bedell
Linn Bishop-Bondestam
Maia Bishop-Bondestam
Josh Crist
Carrie Dean
Harper Dilts
Berkeley Fial
Maddie Filderman
Sarah Gager
Michael Head

Maddy Hemmeter
Thomas Irvine
Nathaniel Johnson
Hunter Jorgensen
Wes Mason
Isa Mazzei
Alexa Pesenti
Annie Saltonstall
Chloe Sens
Abbey Yaron